Written With Love

ANNA-LIESE PRINCE

Icons Media Publishing

WRITTEN WITH LOVE

This book is dedicated to young children and adults. I know that you are eager to find your talents, but please don't rush. You are loved, and you will get there.

With love,
Anna-liese Prince

About The Author

Hi, my name is Anna-liese Prince and I am nine years old. This is the very first book that I have written, and I am so very excited to introduce it to the world. I wanted to let you know a little bit about me, not only as a new author, but a person; a very wonderful little person. Well, not that little, as I am growing up super-fast, but my mummy said that I am still little; so, I guess we will leave it at that. I am currently in year five, and I have been experiencing home schooling over the past year, due to the pandemic with Covid 19. I have been working super hard at home, especially in maths.

Let me just start off by saying that I absolutely love maths, not only because it is very interesting, but also because I get to learn so many new things; like algebra. After being introduced to algebra, I found it super easy, just like everything else to do with maths. I really enjoy maths, and when I grow up, I would like to be a paediatrician and a very successful writer. I would like to give back to the world, take care of children like my mother took care of me, and to ensure that I have the right skills to make my dreams come true. Now that I have introduced myself, let me explain how I started to write my very own poetry book. The reason that I started writing this book was because my mother and father really helped and supported me. One day while I was on google classroom with my school, at Lovelace Primary School, I wrote a poem and submitted it to my school teacher, she then gave me a wonderful feedback; and I was absolutely blown away. I then read the poem to my mother, and may I add, I read it to her while she was in the shower.

Yep, I was actually so excited, I couldn't wait until she came out. My mother was stunned when she finally managed to listen to my poem properly, she really couldn't believe that I wrote it; so I made her listen to my school teachers' response. Mummy then inspired me to write more. She told me how much of an amazing writer I was; and I was encouraged to keep writing. That same day, I wrote six different poems, and from that day on my mother was convinced of my talents, which may I add, prompted our family to publish this book.

I know, I know, weird story right. You just never know when your talents will pop out and hit you in the face. Thank you very much for reading and supporting my brand-new book. I look forward to writing a million more.

With love,
Annaliese Prince

Published by Icons Media Publishing in 2021

Copyright © Anna-liese Prince 2021

First Edition
The author asserts the moral right under the Copyright, Designs and Patents Act 1988 to be identified as the author of this work.
All Rights reserved. No part of this publication may be reproduced, stored in a retrieval system or transmitted, in any form or by any means without the prior consent of the author, nor be otherwise circulated in any form of binding or cover other than that in which it is published and without a similar condition being imposed on the subsequent purchaser.

CONTENTS

Dedication	iv
About The Author	v
The Moon	1
My Skin	3
Bullying	6
Mental Health	9
Mother	12
Different Dads	14
Pets	17
Love	20
Friends	22
Lockdown	24

Evil	27
Water & Food	29
Life & Death	32
Home Schooling	35
Jokes	37
Life	40
Kindness	43
Beauty	45
Family	48
When I Grow Up	50
Who Inspires Me?	53
If I Was an Animal	56
How I See Myself	58
My Talents	61
My Favourite Colour	64

The Weather	67
Dreams	69
Music	71
Crying	74
Regrets	77

The Moon

We observe the moon as a circle, but think nothing as we sleep peacefully,
The moon is concealed, as a new day starts and awaits, until it ends.

~

As midnight arrives, we discover her beauty,
She looks down at us, while she herself is lonely.

~

The moon laughs, as she obliterates behind the clouds,
We see her as just a circle, but nevertheless; she loves us dearly.

~

Once midnight comes, she swoops down to replace the sun,
She glimmers and shines, as we look upon her magnificent elegance.

~

She smiles, with a tear upon her face,
As the sun emerge, it is replaced by the moon,
For a new day has arise.

The Moon

My Skin

Not everyone likes my skin colour,
But I think it is very important,
As it shows the history of my ancestors,
And that alone says it all.

~

My people have cried,
Years and years, we have sacrificed and died,
But one thing we will never do, is hide,
As our history will live on forever,
No matter how much they have tried.

~

My skin colour is the thing, that brings us together,
So, for that alone, people should respect it,
The racism, the hurt,
They judge us so much,
It is almost like a curse.

~

Times like these are horrible,

We are dying left, right and centre,
But, if they really got to know us,
They would realise how much we are loving and tender.

~

But you all need to know,
How much we have been through,
We all need to learn, that life is not what you might think it is.

~

My skin colour brings out the good and bad in people,
And no matter what I do, they will always treat me like a beetle.

WRITTEN WITH LOVE — 5

My skin

Bullying

Bullying is the hurt you give,
It's the way you've been brought up,
It's what you've seen,
It's the life, you've lived.

~

You must know and understand that people may not like it,
And it breaks people's hearts,
But I guess that doesn't stop you; from tearing lives apart.

~

Some kids do it,
But, do they learn it from their parents?
No wonder why some people,
Had gone into disappearance.

~

I know you might say,
"Some people deserve it,"
But that doesn't mean, your actions are worth it.

~

Some people have experienced bullying,
They have lived it all their lives,
It has devastatingly affected them,
They grow up, but their minds are in overdrive.

~

They may not forgive you,
But you can always try,
Since forgiveness is all, they wanted,
But you just have to keep pushing and apply.

Bullying

Mental Health

Okay, so let's talk about mental health,
It breaks down your mind,
While you lose all your wealth.

~

I know this, because my father; has been through it,
He lost his job and home, he thought that he blew it.

~

He was sick and he couldn't think clearly,
He was really stressed out, probably felt a little teary,
Which for me, this experience; have been really scary,
I didn't see him for months, he lost weight and got hairy.

~

I didn't get to see him, when times were very rough,
And please believe me when I say, that this is not a bluff.

~

He was in a mental health hospital, for a very long time,

But in my heart, he will always be mine.

~

These times were very hard,
But he was still loving and supportive,
He fought through his struggles, and he never felt abortive.

Mental Health

Mother

She watches us grow, as they feel a grudge towards her,
But we don't know how much she sacrifice.

~

She recognizes and understands every fight we've had,
But she is determined, to protect us at all costs.

~

She gets lost in our thoughts,
Destroyed, by our minds,
Ruined, by our lives,
And forgotten, in our hearts.

~

We miss her dearly,
As her gratitude and glorious beauty, shines down upon us,

~

She is invisible,
As she lies fulfilled, with a smile, in her grave.

Mother

Different Dads

Today, we are going to be talking about, different dads,
The way they treat their children is just very bad,
But we don't know about their childhood,
It's probably very sad,
Children are broken deep inside,
Which is why, they get mad.

~

Good dads, are really very nice,
They will sacrifice a lot for you,
Even help you, with your life.

~

They are big, bold and strong,
They will protect you, from their ex-wives.
Even though this may be hard,
And the children sometimes, have to pay the price.

~

Now, special dads are the ones we love the most,

They wake up early in the morning, to make their kids the best toast.
~

They are fantastic cooks,
And they always make a good roast,
They even protect their kids at night,
From the scariest ghost.

Different Dads

Pets

They keep us company,
As we cry ourselves to sleep.
Our feelings are crushed, when they die,
But we have already, fallen too deep.

~

They could be a cat, dog or a domestic sheep,
But once we fall in love with them,
They are ours to keep.

~

They think we don't remember,
That we bought them in December,
But we will never forget, all the things that had happened.

~

A new day approaches, but we never forget to visit them,
As they become a pebble in the ground,
Even so, we will never forget their sound.

~

You try to not cry,
As you remember your pet plays,
You remember their gaze,
Love your pet, and ensure there will be no more delays.

Pets

Love

We think love is a chore,
As we take advantage of it every day.

~

We look, in the mist of love,
looking for our true love,
But never identify, the true love within ourselves.

~

As we lie drowning in love,
We see our future,
But we fail to realise that love, **IS** the future.

~

When everything is bad,
Love will destroy it,
As love is our saviour,
Hiding in the dark.

Love

Friends

Friends do not always get appreciated,
As sometimes, friends are irresponsible.

~

For friends can sometimes sacrifice themselves for you,
They will travel around the world, just for you,
Send hugs and kisses just to you,
And when there are no family, they will be there for you.

~

Sometimes they might cry,
Sometimes they might lie,
But you sure don't wish they would ever die.

~

Friends can help you through some rough times,
Even when they prefer to not stay inline.
Forgive but never forget,
Please, always watch the signs,
And love them always,
As we forget this, sometimes.

Friends

Lockdown

Everybody hates it,
As it has caused us so much pain and anguish.

~

Nobody wants it to exist,
But if we don't stay inside,
Bodies, will persists.

~

Lockdown is the only thing, that's keeping us safe,
Even if we are lonely,
No, you are not allowed to see friends or family,
And will think, `If only`.

~

But at least you are not dying coldly,
With a temperature and a cough,
As your skin deteriorates, slowly.

~

Not to worry, you can still video call them,
At least this, we can be thankful for.

~

Many of us, would not be alive today,
And if it wasn't for lock down, there would be no play.

Lockdown

Evil

Evil may scare you,
Or perhaps, make you empowered,
As evil people are cowards,
Evil kills, betrays and is never inspired.

~

Always remember that,
You and evil will always be different,
As you and the people you love,
Will always know the difference.

~

Let's all try to escape the evil within,
As being evil is a choice.

~

A choice that some people can't choose,
As it may be your destiny to be evil,
But you should always try to escape,
And ensure that your loved ones, will always be free from evil.

Evil

Water & Food

Water and food, is the reason we're alive,
Water and food are the reason, life was created,
But water and food are one of the main reasons people are dying,
Tied up and abandoned, as the babies are rejected and crying.

~

Water and food are the reason people are poor,
Just shoved in a corner,
While their cuts and bruises stay sore.

~

Water and food are the reason people are dehydrated,
Left with no family, feeling frustrated.
Water and food are the reason we get discriminated,
As the rich stays rich and more poor people are created.

~

Water and food is the reason, we are getting germs,
But nevertheless, water and food help us to stay alive,
It's what helps us thrive.

~

Water and food, helps us to make things,
We need water and food,
Because if we don't get it, what will we do?

Water & Food

Life & Death

We may not take it seriously,
But life and death is very important.

~

While life may give up on you,
Death can be determined, by how you live your life.
Whether you're a chain smoker or an alcoholic,
A rich man, or attending the right college,
Your future may be destined, by whatever is in your wallet.

~

Life will give you a time, until your death,
Because, you don't appreciate life,
Well, not as much as you appreciate other things,
Like playing games, hurting people and doing all the wrong things.

~

Life and death can both help society,
But that all really depends, on your actions and personality,
As they are both the reason why we do things,

But then again, they are the reason, why some people hold all the strings.

~

Death and life may be terrifying,
But there is always someone around you, who can help.
Someone to protect and guide you, and keep you in good health.

Life & Death

Home Schooling

Time is moving,
As I sit here, enjoying home schooling.

~

It is a lot of hard work, but we are still grooving,
But really who are we fooling?
Since this lock down, we don't know what we are doing.
But children are still blooming.

~

I've learnt algebra, I've learnt about converting money,
I've learnt about decimals, but no matter what, I'm still funny.

~

I've learnt long division, I've even learnt fractions,
And now, I have learnt to think, about my actions.

Home Schooling

Jokes

You may not always hear them,
But I love telling jokes,
People will start complaining,
But I don't listen to those folks.

~

Because laughter is a birth right,
When I do it, I do it with delight,
I can tell my jokes, day and night,
Because I am funny,
And I am the light.

~

You love jokes and you think they're funny,
But, some people don't,
Because they think humour requires money,
Hence why they're poop, are always runny.

~

Laughing and joking is what brings us together,
Every time you laugh,
Your friends, family and others may laugh with you.

~

As laughter and jokes makes life so much brighter,
It hides this life away, from all the dangerous disasters.

Jokes

Life

Life is not a game,
As life is the thing that keeps us sane,
Life is what you gain,
You build and build,
Until you reach in that expensive airplane.

~

Life is like a dream,
Even though it will put you down and make you scream.

~

Life should not be a chore,
Because at times, it can make you bored.

~

We all love to live life,
But some would rather not,
As life can make you broken,
So, it really depends on the one that **YOU**, have chosen.

~

Always remember; life is not the problem,
Life is how we live it, and blossom.

Life

Kindness

We all need kindness,
Because, that is what makes the world a better place,
With all its brightness.

~

Kindness is the thing that helps us along the way,
Kindness helps us when we are lonely,
Kindness helps us when we have nothing,
Even when we get a kind compliment, and start blushing.

~

Kindness is the reason we all exist,
We take advantage of kindness every day,
But really, we should all be spreading kindness,
As kindness loves us, but most of us don't love kindness.

Kindness

Beauty

Beauty, is the reason some people might like you,
Your long hair and facial features,
They like you even more, when you become global leaders.

~

Beauty might be a reason, why people get bullied,
For beauty, may be amazing,
People will stop and stare,
Some might even start gazing.

~

But beauty doesn't change your life,
I mean, it might,
When it comes to modelling and going through hard times.

~

Having beauty means, people might use you,
Beauty is the reason some of you are heartbroken,
Because you never see beyond the beauty,
All you saw was a straight nose, green eyes and a beautiful body.

~

Beauty is buried on the inside,
Some people had to learn this the hard way,
Now, into a ugly future they shall ride.

~

There is beauty inside everyone,
Not having beauty might get you judged,
But at least you won't live the rest of your life,
Holding a grudge.

Beauty

Family

Well, I don't know about yours,
But my family is amazing,
I mean, they are sometimes rude,
And to be honest, I've got my favourite.

~

I do love my uncle Imari, and I do like Chevan,
But nobody comes close, to my mother and dad.

~

I know my family loves me,
But sometimes they don't say it,
But really, they don't have to,
It's their actions that shows it.

~

Family might not always be there for you,
But try your best to be there for them,
Even if they break you down,
Always remember, that they are your family; so please forgive them.

Family

When I Grow Up

When I grow up, I want to be a paediatrician,
Not a beautician,
Or a technician.

~

I want to look after children,
Who are in the worse conditions,
If they get sick,
I want to be their personalized clinician.

~

When I grow up, I want to be a writer,
I want to make my future, so much more brighter.

~

When I grow up, I want to be famous and wealthy,
But most importantly, I want to be really healthy.

~

When I grow up, I want to help people,

Making the world a better place,
   Protecting it, from evil.

When I Grow Up

Who Inspires Me?

The person that inspires me the most, is my mother,
She inspires me because, she is like no other,
She takes care of me and she isn't very mean,
She wears her crown proudly, as she is my queen.

~

She inspires me because, she is so nice,
She looks out for me,
And she always gives the best advice.

~

She's a great cook,
Even better when she cooks rice,
Her love is so special,
It's like dancing on ice.

~

My mother is very interesting,
And when I grow older, she is definitely going to be worth visiting.

~

I love my mother,
And I just want to thank her, for everything that she has done for me.

Who Inspires Me

If I Was an Animal

If I was an animal, I would be a cat,
Even though they sometimes, act like a brat.

~

They will scratch you and fight,
Even try to spat,
But they are loving little creatures,
They might even sit and have a chat.

~

They are intelligent,
And they always, land on their feet,
And when they do something special,
They always want a treat,

~

They are fluffy, and cute,
Their fur, is always so neat,
They will kill you, with kisses,
And boy, do they like to eat.

If I Was An Animal

How I See Myself

I used to see myself as an ugly person,
But some people may say that I am not,

~

I see myself as a hard-working business girl,
But some people see me as a child.

~

I see myself as a good person,
But some people might disagree,
But who really cares?
When I grow up, I'll be standing taller than a tree.

~

I see myself as a great person at maths,
I'm only nine years old,
But I am ready to sit the SATs.

~

I think that, I will be a very successful; when I grow up,

That's right, because I will work hard to reach to the top,
I will not allow my struggles, to overflow in my cup,
And I will try harder, to make my business start-up.

~

Some people might bully me for my success,
But the reason I'm so successful, is because of my parents,
They are loving and smart,
But most importantly, they are very caring.

How I See Myself

My Talents

So, you want to know how I felt, when I discovered my talents?
It was like floating on the stars,
Trying to find, my own balance.

~

It was very great,
I felt excited,
Just young, strong and delighted.
It's like my heart said, there you go Anna,
But don't be frightened.

~

Some people may be jealous,
Because this might not be, what they wanted,
But these are my talents,
And I will never feel haunted.

~

I love the fact, that I have discovered my talents,
And for this I am very grateful,
I just hope that my friends, don't find this painful,

~

Everyone has talents,
Even if you can't see it,
It's in your blood,
You just have to, believe in it.

My Talents

My Favourite Colour

All colours are very pretty,
But my favourite colour is better,
I just love the colour pink,
It's like wearing, my favourite pink sweater.

~

Some people think, that colours are sometimes boring,
But colours are all around us,
And that's what keeps us going,
Shining, as our light; just keeps on glowing.

~

There's beauty in colour,
And that's something we don't realize,
It's that feeling when you hold your head up,
And stare into the deep blue skies.

~

When it comes to colour,
It is no joke,
It's like having a green-eyed friend,

Watching, as they awoke.

~

Colour makes us different,
Look at the colour of people,
Feeling the freedom of our own colours,
It's like staring, at a flying Eagle.

My Favourite Colour

The Weather

I do love the weather,
But it can be pretty unpredictable,
It can be sunny one minute,
Then, it will rain all day,
And make us miserable.

~

In England, the rain is always bad,
People are unable to go outside,
Which makes us, very sad.

~

It will snow, it will hail,
And we only get sun, like once a month,
I wish I was those people,
Sitting by the lake front.

~

When it comes to England weather,
It's always pretty bad,
It's just cold, disgusting and lonely,
All around pretty sad.

The Weather

Dreams

Dreams are amazing,
Especially, when they are good dreams,
That feeling, of dreaming about water,
Floating, down a stream.

~

Dreams are the things, that encourage us, to do our best,
Because this life, is just like playing chest,
It's hard, things can get difficult,
And sometimes feels like a pest,
But you just have to put your mind to it,
And do your very best.

~

You can get the things you want,
If you just believe in yourself,
Never give up dreaming,
Especially, if you want to go into public speaking.

Dreams

Music

Music is fantastic,
But, that's not the real reason why I like it,
I like it because, music brings us together,
Even when there are stormy weathers.

~

Music is life,
We live, breathe and cherish music,
You can discover hip hop or soul,
Whichever one you chooses.

~

Without music life would be really boring,
Sitting down playing games, not even exploring,
So that's why we should keep adoring,
Turn that music on while you brush your teeth,
Go on, enjoy your morning.

~

Always remember,
Music is the thing that we hear every day,

That could be on T.V,
Or on a computer, as you play.

~

Music will play, as you dance and enjoy your birthday,
And you never know, maybe one day, you will make it to Broadway.

Music

Crying

Tears were falling down my face,
As I watched a movie, about human race,
The respect of people, is what they were trying to chase,
Even when they could barely, get a date.

~

They were flying in a house filled with balloons,
Yes, they were trying to reach to space,
His wife died,
So, silence and peace, was what he chased.

~

I don't know why I started crying,
I don't know how it happened in the first place,
But it really touched my heart,
Because the movie was filled, with beauty and grace.

~

To me, this movie was no game,
But when it comes to this, who really was to blame?
When he was hurting, nobody even came,

But then again, people are just pretty lame,
This movie broke my heart, oh boy; what a shame.

Crying

Regrets

Regrets are the things that allows us to learn from our mistakes,
It's like falling in love, then having a heart break.
It's also like getting fat, when you're over there eating a cheesecake,
You only regret it once you're done,
Then you hide in disgrace.

~

So that's one reason, why we hate to have regrets,
And that's probably why we need to stop making bets,
You will live your life, drowning in debts,
And that's when regret, will start to become a threat.

~

Yes, there's all types of regrets,
There's leaving your pet alone, as it falls and dies out of its nest,
When really you should have thought about getting it to the vet,
But no, you had people, waiting to be met.

~

Lastly, never use your regrets against people,
Because karma, is going to ruin your chances, without reason.

www.ingramcontent.com/pod-product-compliance
Lightning Source LLC
Chambersburg PA
CBHW071536080526
44588CB00011B/1691